HIGH-TECH SCIENCE AT HOME

How Do Smart Homes Work?

by Agnieszka Biskup

CAPSTONE PRESS
a capstone imprint

Capstone Captivate is published by Capstone Press, an imprint of Capstone.
1710 Roe Crest Drive
North Mankato, Minnesota 56003
www.capstonepub.com

Library of Congress Cataloging-in-Publication Data is available on the Library of Congress website.
ISBN: 978-1-4966-8072-3 (library binding)
ISBN: 978-1-4966-8714-2 (paperback)
ISBN: 978-1-4966-8168-3 (eBook PDF)

Summary: Imagine you arrive at school and realize you forgot to feed the dog. No problem. Pull out your phone and command the dog dish to dispense a serving of food. That's all there is to it—if you live a smart home. What once sounded like science fiction is now a reality for some families. People use smart phones and other devices to lock doors, turn on lights, close window shades, and check to see how much milk they have in the fridge. Find out how this technology works and what the future holds for smart homes.

Image Credits
AP Photo: 11; Flickr: phylevn, 13; Getty Images: Chip Somodevilla, 28, Frederic J. Brown, 38, GraphicaArtis, 10, Maskot, 5, Mint, 27, The Museums, Galleries and Archives of Wolverhampton, 7, Stringer/David Becker, 40, T3 Magazine, 17, Tap Magazine, 21, WAVE: Museum of Science and Industry, Chicago, 8; iStockphoto: alvarez, 18, hakule, 23; Newscom: Cover Images/Eight Sleep, 25, Cover Images/Ori, Inc./Dean Murray, 41, IFTN/United Archives, 9, picture-alliance/dpa/Armin Weigel, 39, picture-alliance/dpa/Oliver Berg, 31, Westend61 GmbH/UWE_UMSTAETTER, 16; Pixabay: Clker-Free-Vector-Images, cover (house icon); Shutterstock: Andrey_Popov, 24, CreativeAngela, 15, Dmi T, 37, Evgeniy Pavlovski, 33, Juan Ci, 19, KooNG_A, 14, leolintang, 42, LIORIKI, background (circuit board), nexusby, cover, Orhan Cam, 6, Phonlamai Photo, 29, Piotr Wawrzyniuk, 35, SkyPics Studio, 44, Zhu Difeng, 26; SuperStock: Caia Images, 20

Editorial Credits
Editor: Leah Kaminski; Designer: Sara Radka; Media Researcher: Eric Gohl; Production Specialist: Kathy McColley

All internet sites appearing in back matter were available and accurate when this book was sent to press.

Printed in the United States
PA117

Table of Contents

Introduction

Imagine walking into your house after school on a snowy day. You don't have to fumble for your keys. The door opens for you automatically. When the door opens, the lights turn on. Your favorite music starts playing softly. You stamp your slushy boots on the mat. Then, your robot mop rolls toward you to clean the mess. A few years ago, this scene might have seemed like something out of science fiction. Today, some homes can do all this and more. It's just your ordinary smart home.

Smart homes use technology to try to make life easier. They use appliances and electronic devices that have tiny computers inside. This helps the appliances communicate with each other and the world around them. You can control these so-called **smart devices** by using a **smartphone** or your voice. You can connect them together so they can communicate with each other. Some of them can learn from you too. These high-tech advances are changing our lives at home.

HIGH-TECH FACT

The term "smart house" was trademarked way back in 1984 by the American National Association of Home Builders. Today, people often use the term "smart home" instead.

Many smart homes are controlled through touchscreen displays.

CHAPTER 1
The History of Smart Homes

People use technology to try and make life easier. Look at what life was like in the 1800s, before electricity was common in homes. You had to scrub your clothes clean on a washing board and hang them on a line to dry. Cooking was done over a wood stove. But first, the wood had to be chopped. People used candles or gas lamps for lighting. Daily chores took a huge amount of time. People who could afford servants had them do all the hard work of running a household. But most people had no servants.

HIGH-TECH FACT
The White House didn't have electricity until 1891.

Children were more involved in housework and other chores in the 1800s.

Electricity in the house would change everything. In the 1880s, small electric power stations were developed in the U.S. They were able to provide power to a few city blocks at a time. Once homes had electric power, the invention of electric home appliances soon followed. Electric vacuum cleaners, washing machines, and ovens made running a home much easier. For those who could afford it, the new technology made life more comfortable.

The House of Tomorrow was made mostly of glass.

People have always thought about what the modern home would and should look like. Once technology became part of life, it became part of the idea for the future home too.

In 1933, the Chicago World's Fair featured a "House of Tomorrow." It had a dishwasher, central air-conditioning, and an airplane hangar.

Popular Mechanics magazine ran an article in 1950 called "Push-Button Manor." In this super modern home, you could open curtains with a touch of a button. If you pressed the doorbell, the porch light would turn on too. At the time, it seemed pretty advanced to most people.

Disneyland opened an exhibit in 1957. The Monsanto House of the Future imagined what the home would be like in 1986. Much of the house was made of plastic. The house had a microwave oven and a hands-free telephone. It also had a sink that would go up and down to match a person's height. Over 20 million visitors saw the exhibit before it closed in 1967.

SMART HOMES IN SCIENCE FICTION

1950 Ray Bradbury writes a short story called "There Will Come Soft Rains." It's about a computer-controlled house that keeps working even after its owners die.

1962 The Jetsons, a cartoon about a family in the future, airs. The family has a robot housekeeper, video calling, and robot vacuum cleaners. The home also has robot arms that come out of the wall to help bathe and dress the family.

1999 "Smart House," a Disney Channel Original Movie, shows a computerized house that begins to take on a personality of its own. It ends up trying to control the family inside to keep it safe.

Computers changed what a house could do even more than electricity did. People began imagining what the house of the future would be like if computers were used in the home. The Philco-Ford Corporation made a promotional film in the 1960s. It promised that a home computer would be many things. It would be a "secretary, librarian, banker, teacher, medical technician, bridge partner, and all-around servant."

One of the first early home computers was the ECHO IV. ECHO stood for "Electronic Computing Home Operator." Jim Sutherland, an **engineer** at Westinghouse Electric, built the ECHO IV in 1966 from scrap computer parts. He built the computer so his wife and children could control their home.

Early smart home inventions relied on buttons and dials.

The ECHO IV made shopping lists, controlled the temperature, and turned appliances on and off. The computer was never made available to the public. Nonetheless, the ECHO IV was still a big step in the development of smart homes.

Jim Sutherland's ECHO IV had several terminals around the house so the family could control it.

CHAPTER 2
Smart Home Technology

Smart homes may have seemed like science fiction, but engineers started making them a reality. Computers started taking a bigger role in how the different parts of a home worked.

The first smart home system that was sold to the public was the X10 system, made by Pico Electronics. It was developed in 1975. The X10 system used the electrical wires in a home to talk to smart devices. It sent signals throughout the house to turn lights on and off and open and close blinds. It could also start or stop appliances and control anything else connected to the system.

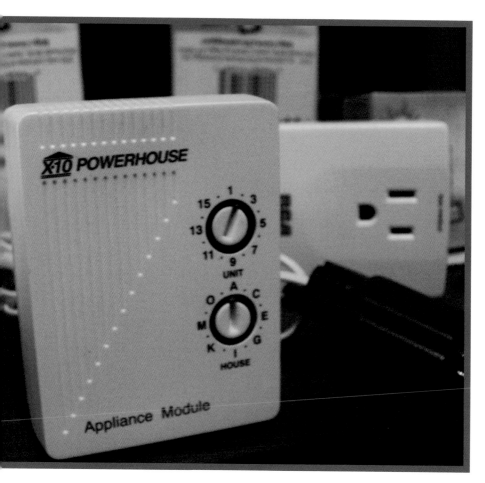

X10 systems need both receivers and transmitters, which come in both wired and plug-in versions.

X10 had some problems. The electrical lines in a home can get "noisy" from powering other devices. An X10 device got confused by this "noise." It sometimes did not understand a command to start. It sometimes even thought the "noise" was a command to stop something. This problem made engineers think. Could devices communicate without using wires at all?

X10 is still used in some homes, but many new smart home systems are now wireless. They use **radio waves** instead of wires to communicate.

Wi-Fi is a way that computers, phones, and other devices can communicate with each other and the internet. They can communicate without wires connecting them together. Radio waves connect the devices to a box called a Wi-Fi **router**. The router acts like a central control hub. This creates a Wi-Fi **network**. Each device can communicate with each other because they are on the same network.

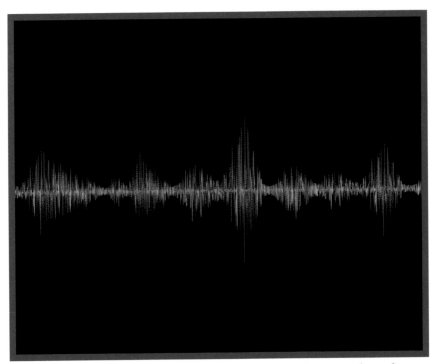

Radio waves are often confused with sound waves, but they are very different. This is an image of a sound wave.

Smart homes can use wireless technologies other than Wi-Fi. The whole idea behind a smart home is to have everything talking to everything else. ZigBee and Z-Wave are different "languages" that your hub and its smart devices can use to "talk" to each other.

What is a radio wave?

A radio wave is an electromagnetic wave, part of a whole family of energy called **electromagnetic radiation**. It includes gamma rays, X-rays, ultraviolet light, visible light, infrared light, microwaves, and radio waves. Visible light is the only form we can see with our eyes. Radio waves are invisible to us and can travel through air and space. Radio waves are used for many types of communication, including mobile phones, radio broadcasting, and Wi-Fi networks.

So how exactly does a smart home work? You can have smart devices around the home that aren't connected to each other. But you can also have a smart home hub that will connect all the smart devices to each other and the internet. The hub is like the brain of your smart home. A hub gives you control over everything by using an **app** on your smartphone or tablet. You can easily communicate with your smart home and its smart devices by using a screen.

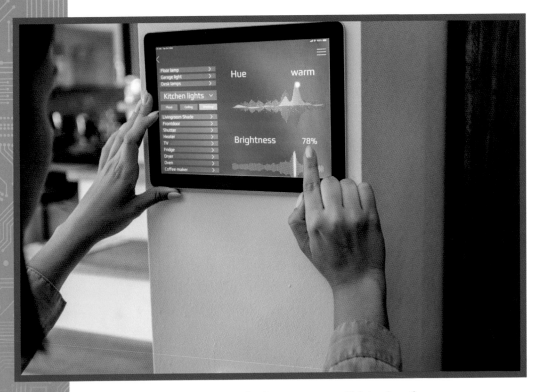

Many newer smart hubs support all kinds of smart home protocols, from ZigBee and Z-Wave to Alexa voice commands.

Smart Sensors

Smart **sensors** are like the eyes and ears of your home. Some smart sensors can sense water on the floor. They'll text your smartphone to tell you about a leak. Contact sensors can tell you if a window is open or if the fridge door isn't closed. Smart sensors can work with other parts of your smart home. For example, you can have your smart lights turn on as you open the front door.

A smart motion sensor can detect motion in an area. It can then send you an alert, trigger a siren, or turn the lights on or off. Some smart motion sensors even have a feature called pet immunity. They won't alert you if they detect motion from a small creature. A maximum pet size is usually listed. One motion detector says it will ignore movement from pets as large as 55 pounds. If you have a Great Dane, you're out of luck!

If you don't want to use a screen to communicate with your smart devices, you can always talk to them instead. Digital assistants like Amazon's Alexa, Apple's Siri, or Google's Assistant let you control smart devices with your voice. These digital assistants are also known as voice assistants. They can understand voice commands and can complete tasks as directed. Some let you schedule routines with your smart devices. For example, if you say "good night," the assistant might turn off the lights and lock the doors. These assistants can, in some cases, take the place of a hub.

It's estimated that there will be 83 million smart speakers or digital assistants used in the United States in 2020.

Amazon's smart products, including Alexa, are some of the
most popular on the market.

Amazingly, these assistants can learn over time
and get to know your habits. They get smarter at
knowing what you want the more you use them. They
can start predicting your requests or suggest things
they think you might like.

Does Alexa Know What You're Saying?

Alexa and Siri don't really understand what you're
saying. But they are always listening. They are listening
for the "wake word" that activates them, like "Alexa" or
"Hey Siri." Once they hear the word that wakes them up,
they start recording what you say. They basically convert
your **audio** into a string of text and compare it to a huge
amount of expected commands. If they find a match, they
follow a set of instructions. If they don't find an exact
match, they look for something close. And if they can't
find a match at all, they'll apologize.

Some smart TVs even have touchscreens.

CHAPTER **3**
Smart Homes Today

Today, millions of people have smart home devices. Take a look at what you can find in a smart living room today.

Smart living rooms have smart TVs. You can **stream** television and movies from Netflix or Hulu. You can also play games, browse the internet, and control your other smart devices.

Smart light bulbs might not sound interesting, but it's pretty cool that you can control them from your smartphone. Philips Hue sells smart bulbs that can give you 16 million different colors.

Thermostats control the temperature in your home. They rely on you to set the temperature in your house. Not the smart Nest Learning Thermostat! It programs itself by learning what temperature you like and builds a schedule around yours. It adjusts the temperature up or down to make you comfortable when you are home. By not being on when you're not home, it will also save energy.

Smart light bulbs are not only fun, but useful. These LED bulbs can last for years.

Your kitchen is already full of electronic appliances and gadgets. In today's smart home they are getting even smarter.

With a smart oven, you can adjust the cooking temperature from an app. You can also turn it off from anywhere using your smartphone.

Samsung makes a smart refrigerator called the Family Hub. It has a camera that lets you see inside it with an app. An assistant is built into the door. It allows you to play music and get reminders.

The GeniCan is a smart trash can. It can scan the barcodes on packaging as you throw it away. They'll be added to a shopping list through the GeniCan app. You'll even get an alert when the can needs to be emptied. (No need for Mom or Dad to remind you!)

Of course, if you don't want to cook, you can always ask Alexa or Siri to order you a pizza.

Smartphone apps are one of the most common ways to control smart home devices.

In the morning, your digital assistant can tell you the weather and news headlines.

Even bedrooms are being made smart. They can help you relax, sleep better, and wake up easier.

When you're ready to go to sleep, you can control your smart lights from the comfort of your bed. If you use smart bulbs, you can adjust the bulb colors to make your bedroom relaxing. You can also create a sunrise effect for when you wake up.

Smart shades are similar to smart lights. You can lower and raise the shades with your phone or voice. With a routine, you can do lots of things at once. By saying "good night," you can dim the lights and lower the shades.

Smart mattresses can track how you sleep. They measure your heart rate and your breathing. The Eight Sleep Pod mattress can adjust its firmness and temperature using feedback from your body. Then in the morning, you can look at your daily sleep report on an app.

Smart mattresses can wake you up in the morning by slowly changing the temperature.

Even the smallest rooms in your home can have smart home technology. After all, who wouldn't want a smart bathroom?

Smart showers, such as the U by Moen, allow you to set the perfect shower temperature. Do you want to shower for exactly five minutes? You can set the shower duration too. You can even use your voice to activate it.

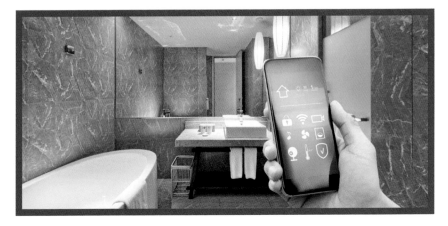

Smart bathrooms have many possiblities. Some showerheads can play music for you.

Smart Art

Meural is a smart digital frame that can access over 30,000 pieces of art. You can change the picture as often as you'd like. Of course, you can also load your own artwork and photos too. Choose and change your art using an app. You can also wave your hand in front of the sensors built into the frame. That motion will change the picture in the frame like magic.

Smart mirrors have sensors that recognize when you enter the room.

Are you bored just looking at your face? A smart mirror will show the time, date, weather, news updates, and any reminders or calendar appointments. Or, because it's also a TV screen, you can always catch an episode of your favorite cartoon instead.

There's even a smart toilet that will flip the seat and lid automatically and flush for you!

Smart security systems are popular in smart homes. You can monitor and control different security devices through an app on your smartphone.

Security cameras allow you to see the outside and inside of your home when you're not there. Motion sensors will turn on lights and an alarm if intruders are detected.

The Nest doorbell uses high-definition video to show you the scene on your doorstep.

Some people use their smart security cameras to keep an eye on their pets when they're away.

Smart video doorbell cameras allow you to see who's at the door even when you're not home. They connect with your home Wi-Fi and alert you when anyone approaches the door. You can talk to visitors using your smartphone and even let them in. The Ring Video Doorbell gives you video coverage of your door even in the dark.

The Nest Hello video doorbell also records video, but it goes one step further. It can recognize faces to detect who is at the door. It can send you a special alert when a friend or family member has arrived. Nest Hello can also tell the difference between a person and a thing. It will send an alert when it spots a package delivery or pickup.

Smart homes can also help take care of the people who live inside them. Sometimes, older people have bad eyesight. They may have poor balance. A fall could be dangerous. Smart technology may help them lead safer lives.

Smart sensors can help monitor movement in the house. They can alert a caregiver if someone might have fallen. Smart sensors can turn on smart lights when someone enters a room. There's no need to look for a light switch, which lessens the risk of tripping.

A contact sensor on a medicine cabinet door can tell how many times it was opened. Digital assistants like Alexa can remind users to take their medication. It can help them refill prescriptions.

Smart Pet Care

Smart homes can also care for pets! Smart pet feeders can calculate the exact amount of food your pet needs. It bases the amount on the pet's age, weight, and activity level. It will then give out the meal portions on schedule. Of course, self-cleaning litter boxes and automatic dog doors exist too.

The Owlet smart sock lets parents check on their baby's health in real time by connecting to an app.

Smart home technology doesn't only help older people. Many parents use smart baby monitors to check in on their baby 24/7. Some of these monitors can even track the baby's heart rate and oxygen levels as they sleep. They will notify parents if something seems wrong.

CHAPTER 4
Robots to the Rescue

We don't have C-3PO just yet, but robots are already part of the smart home.

Probably the most famous smart home robot is iRobot's Roomba, the robot vacuum cleaner. It was first introduced in 2002. You can connect the newest version, the Roomba S9+, to the Roomba app and your home Wi-Fi too.

The Roomba S9+ is meant to work with a robot mop called the Braava Jet m6, also by iRobot. Since both the Roomba S9+ and the Braava speak to the same iRobot app, they'll coordinate to clean your floors. When the Roomba finishes vacuuming, it signals the Braava that it's time to mop. Pretty sweet teamwork!

Cleaning windows is a pain, but the Alfawise Magnetic Window Cleaning Robot can help. It comes with a remote control that directs where the robot goes. You can also use a smartphone app and even select different cleaning modes.

The Roomba is one of the oldest smart home devices. One million units were sold by 2004.

Smart robots can do a lot. If you have a smart home, why not have a smart yard too? Hate cutting the lawn? Automated lawn mowers like the Worx Landroid will take care of it for you. Need to clean the pool? The Dolphin Nautilus robot will use GPS to make sure the job is completely done.

Or maybe you want a robot security guard? After all, your smart security cameras can't see everything. The Appbot Riley 2.0 patrols your house to make sure everything is safe. It has a night vision camera and motion detectors. Riley will send alerts to your phone if it sees anything suspicious. Riley also has a built-in microphone so you can hear what it hears too.

Ubtech Lynx is a 20-inch-tall robot that is supposed to help Amazon's Alexa come alive. Lynx can recognize faces and will follow you around the house. It can also dance and teach you some basic yoga. And, of course, it makes shopping lists for when you need to place an Amazon order.

Smart mowers have safety sensors, and you can always
locate and control the mower from your phone.

CHAPTER 5
Even Smarter Homes (Smart Homes in the Future)

Engineers are working on even more ways to make houses truly smart. One thing some of them are working on is called the Internet of Things. Basically this is all about connecting all the everyday objects around us to the internet. It gives these objects a "brain," just like our smartphones and computers. This allows the objects to "talk" to each other and act intelligently. They can collect information about when and how you use them. They can learn what you want and when you need it.

The Internet of Things is already here, but it's expected to become even bigger in the years to come. Sensors will be in everything from your toothbrush to your tennis shoes. And they'll all be talking about you behind your back. In the future, your smart health monitor will talk to your smart refrigerator. It might suggest healthier food choices if you're not feeling well!

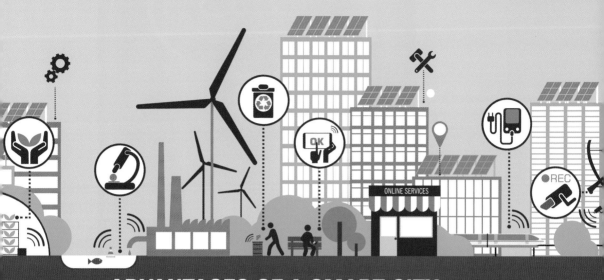

ADVANTAGES OF A SMART CITY

In a smart city, you could access important services 24 hours a day, and even the street lights could be smart.

Smart Cities

In the future, there won't just be smart homes, but entire smart cities. Imagine an entire city lit by smart lamps that can adapt to the weather. Waste will be collected only when garbage bins' sensors say they're full. Sensors on water pipes and tanks will alert people to leaks. A smart city will hopefully be safer and more efficient.

Mykie is also designed to be entertaining.

Developments in robotics will make today's smart home even smarter. Some are already in the works.

Mykie, short for "My Kitchen Elf," is a kitchen assistant robot. Mykie plans your meals by connecting to a network of home appliances. It can help you find recipes based on what you have in the fridge. As you start cooking, the robot will preheat the oven to the right temperature. Mykie will also hook you up to cooking classes in real time to help teach you to cook.

Nvidia, a computer-graphics company, is working on a robotic arm that helps with kitchen cleanup. It will also slice and dice your food, as long as you're not worried about giving a robot a knife.

Have you thought about having robot furniture move itself around on your command? Ori Living is working on furniture that changes according to your needs. For example, it can get your bed out of the way when you need a desk. All of Ori Living's products can be controlled using voice commands or through an app.

Smart home products like the Ori Studio will allow people to live more functionally in small spaces.

Health will be a huge part of the future smart home. Imagine looking in a mirror that can run a quick health check on your skin. A bed equipped with health sensors will tell you if you're showing signs of being sick. Cameras and sensors in the fridge will suggest healthy foods. Medicine cabinets will check if you've taken your pills. Toilets will sample your urine to check for disease.

Smart refrigerators can tell you when you're out of certain foods, and the touchscreen doors can even let you leave notes for your family.

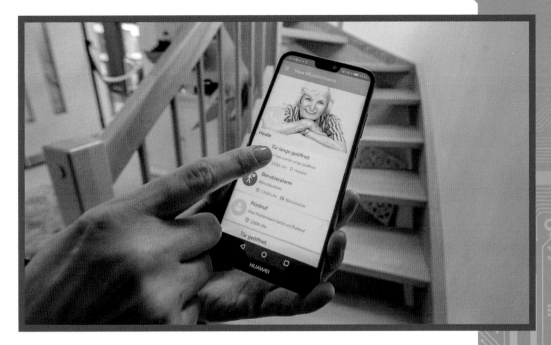

Many nursing homes are already using smart devices like lights, thermostats, and digital assistants.

Robots may provide even more help to senior citizens in the future. Scientists hope robots can help take care of people in nursing homes. RAS is a robot created by Washington State University scientists. RAS (short for Robot Activity Support System) uses sensors in a smart home to determine where the residents are in the house. The sensors let the robot know what the residents are doing and whether they need any help. RAS can navigate through rooms to find people on its own. It can lead residents to the kitchen for a snack or to their medications.

> **HIGH-TECH FACT**
> Medical alert systems have been around for some time. Life Alert, for example, was founded in 1987.

There have already been some cases of hackers taking over smart home devices.

Smart homes promise to make life better. But they also have problems.

People worry about privacy. For example **hackers** could take control of a smart home's cameras to spy on families. They could turn off a home's alarms and unlock the doors. Burglars could then break in.

Many people are also worried about privacy. After all, digital assistants are listening to everything they say.

Problems with privacy and hacking still need to be worked out. However, it's likely that you'll be living in a smart home one day, if you are not already. Homes today are being built smart from the start. Experts say smart home technology will be as common as indoor plumbing.

Predicting the future can be tricky. We don't know exactly what a smart home of the future will be like. But you can bet the home you live in today will seem old-fashioned by comparison.

Smart Home Innovations

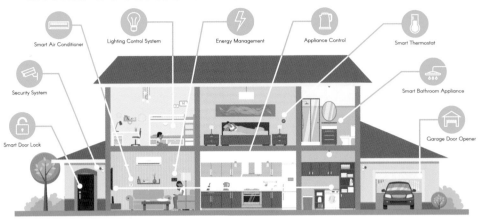

Smart Garage Door Opener

An app on your phone can open the garage door as you approach it, even sensing that your phone is approaching. You can also close the garage door from work if you forgot to close it, or open it remotely so a neighbor can borrow your lawn mower.

Smart Lighting System

These systems control lamps through smart bulbs. You can adjust the brightness and the color. They can also detect when lights are failing.

Smart Thermostat

Smart thermostats control temperature based on who is home, what time of day it is, and what room you are in. You can access and control the thermostat through an app on your phone if you want to change it.

Smart Air Conditioner

A smart air conditioner has a lot of the same features as the smart thermostat. It also has sensors that turn the unit off when a window or door is open.

Smart Door Lock

With a smart door lock, you can lock or unlock your door from an app on your device. You can set the door to unlock when your phone approaches. You can even set it to let certain people in at only certain times. Having a party? Let people on the guest list in, and no one else.

Smart Energy Use

Your smart home uses a lot of energy from gas and electricity. Smart energy management systems monitor and control your energy use across the entire house. That will make you more energy efficient.

Smart Appliances

Refrigerators, ovens, coffee pots, toasters, and more. New smart appliances hit the market every year. They can be used on their own or with a smart home hub.

Smart Security System

Smart security systems can contact authorities when an alarm is set off. They allow you to remotely access and control locks, security cameras, video doorbells, and more.

Smart Bathrooms

Smart bathrooms can include smart mirrors and toilets. The pressure and temperature of the water can also be controlled. Certain temperatures can be set for certain times. For example, maybe you like a hot bath at night and a cooler shower in the morning. You can control it all from your device.

GLOSSARY

app (AP)—a computer program that performs a certain task; short for application

audio (AW-dee-oh)—sound humans can hear

electromagnetic radiation (i-lek-troh-mag-NET-ik ray-dee-AY-shuhn)—waves of energy that can be visible or invisible

engineer (en-juh-NEER)—someone who uses science to design things

hacker (HAK-ur)—a person who illegally gains access to a computer system

network (NET-wurk)—a system of two or more devices connected to each other

radio wave (RAY-dee-oh WAYV)—an electromagnetic wave used in radio, television, or radar communication

router (ROUT-ur)—a device that collects signals from other devices and then sends the signals to the internet (or vice versa)

sensor (SEN-sur)—an instrument that detects physical changes in the environment

smart device (SMART di-VYS)—an electronic gadget that can connect, interact, and share with its user and other smart devices

smartphone (SMART-fohn)—a cell phone that includes additional functions like an internet browser

stream (STREEM)—a steady flow of information; a steady flow of data

Wi-Fi (WAI-fai)—technology that allows computers to communicate with each other wirelessly

READ MORE

Biskup, Agnieszka. *The Remarkable World of Robots: Max Axiom STEM Adventures.* North Mankato, MN: Capstone Press, 2018.

Schutten, Jan Paul. *Hello from 2030: The Science of the Future and You.* New York: Alladin, 2014.

Wainewright, Max. *Scratch Code: Smart Homes.* New York: Crabtree Publishing Company, 2019.

INTERNET SITES

How Stuff Works
https://home.howstuffworks.com/smart-home.htm

Kids Discover
https://www.kidsdiscover.com/teacherresources/all-about-robots/

National Geographic
https://www.nationalgeographic.org/interactive/challenge-robots/

Technology for Kids
https://www.funkidslive.com/podcast/techno-mum-technology-engineering-for-kids/

INDEX